CHRONICLING
CIVIL RESISTANCE

ICNC PRESS

Chronicling Civil Resistance

by Deborah Mathis
and Hailey Grace Allen 2021

Published by ICNC Press

This publication was funded in part by a
grant from Humanity United (HU). The opinions
expressed are those of the author and do
not necessarily reflect the views of HU.

International Center on Nonviolent Conflict

600 New Hampshire Ave NW, Suite 710
Washington, D.C. 20037 USA
www.nonviolent-conflict.org

CONTACT: icnc@nonviolent-conflict.org

ISBN: 978-1-943271-46-7

CHRONICLING
CIVIL RESISTANCE

THE JOURNALISTS' GUIDE TO UNRAVELING
AND REPORTING NONVIOLENT STRUGGLES
FOR RIGHTS, FREEDOM AND JUSTICE

CONTENTS

"The market for violence is drying up."

INTRODUCTION

Civil resistance plays a critical role in the development, enactment, and evolution of democratic societies. All over the world, from remote hamlets to burgeoning cities, aggrieved and oppressed people are organizing to demand remedies for wrongs they suffer at the hands of powerful governments, corporations, organizations, and institutions. Increasingly, these people are choosing to engage in nonviolent tactics such as strikes, boycotts, mass protests, and other acts of noncooperation.

A 2020 study published in the *Journal of Democracy* found there were more civil resistance campaigns worldwide between 2010 and 2019 than in any other decade since 1900.[1] Although some of these campaigns have been marred by acts of injury or destruction, often by peripheral actors, the study notes that "The market for violence is drying up."

With the global proliferation of civil resistance, an increasing number of journalists are looking beyond the surface of crowd sizes and clashes with police to inform their reporting. Many have shown a talent and determination for more comprehensive and contextual coverage — a welcome development for journalism and public awareness.

This guide is intended to deepen understanding of the nuances of movements, campaigns, and strategies that employ a range of nonviolent tactics to exert power. *Chronicling Civil Resistance* is intended for reporters, producers, editors, news talk show hosts and other news professionals who want to deepen their analysis and advance their reporting of civil resistance activity from conception to aftermath.

This manual was written by ICNC's Director of Communications Deborah Mathis, a retired veteran journalist whose career included stints as reporter, anchor, editor, syndicated columnist, White House correspondent and journalism educator; and Hailey Grace Allen, a former journalist and Ph.D. candidate in Media and Communications at the Hussman School, University of North Carolina, Chapel Hill. ICNC President & CEO Hardy Merriman also contributed to this work, providing input and editorial feedback.

We hope you find it useful.

Increasingly, journalists are looking beyond crowd sizes and clashes with police to inform their reporting.

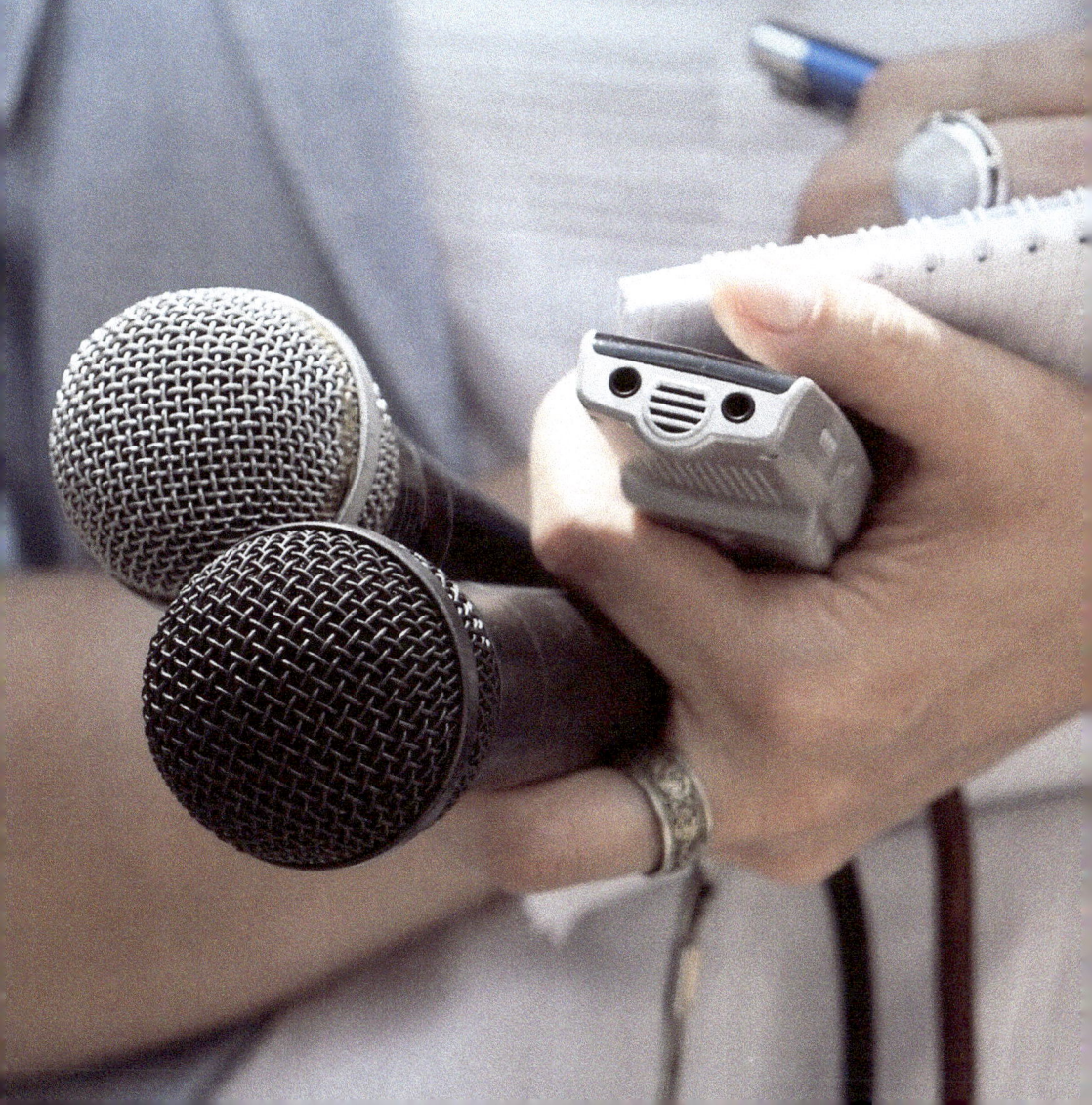

DEFINING CIVIL RESISTANCE: WHAT IT IS AND IS NOT

THE FIRST WORD in "civil resistance" has a two-fold meaning: (1) citizen-driven or citizen-related; and (2) nonviolent. You may find that some refer to "nonviolent civil resistance" to underscore the nature of the action. However, activists, organizers and scholars increasingly use "civil resistance" when referring to the powerful way ordinary people fight for rights, freedom, justice, and self-determination without using violence.

Large-scale, peaceful demonstrations are the most familiar acts of civil resistance, but they are far from the only ones. The late sociologist Gene Sharp famously identified 198 methods of civil resistance in his seminal 1973 work, *The Politics of Nonviolent Action*.[2] These myriad methods generally fall into one of two categories:

Commission or Omission

1. **Acts of commission,** in which people do things they are not supposed to do, not expected to do, or are forbidden to do. Examples include:
   - Protest demonstrations
   - Blockades
   - Occupying buildings or public spaces
   - Civil disobedience (such as refusing to disperse or resisting arrest)

2. **Acts of omission,** in which people do not do things they are supposed to do, expected to do, or required to do. Examples include:
   - Labor strikes
   - Consumer boycotts
   - Work slowdowns
   - Divestment
   - Other acts of noncooperation that generate social, economic, or political pressure

A common misperception about this phenomenon is that its practitioners must be morally and philosophically committed to nonviolence, much as Mohandas Gandhi and Dr. Martin Luther King, Jr. adopted nonviolence as the lodestar of their lives.

However, people of diverse ethical views practice civil resistance as a *strategic choice*. They commit to remaining nonviolent because it holds pragmatic advantages for them in achieving their goals. This is a critical distinction.

Nonviolent campaigns
had more than twice the
success rate of armed
insurrections.

THE LOGIC OF
CIVIL RESISTANCE

VIOLENCE IS COMMONLY assumed to be the strongest force by which a population can confront oppressive governments. But this stubborn conventional wisdom has been proven wrong by more than 100 years of data. Civil resistance creates an asymmetric conflict with governments, in which a population has greater advantages than it would in armed conflict. Most governments are equipped to handle violent challenges but are seldom prepared to handle organized noncooperation by their populations. The historical record and empirical data show that nonviolent movements have a much higher probability of achieving their goals and democratic outcomes and consolidating gains than do their violent counterparts.

Underscoring this break with conventional wisdom, a groundbreaking and comprehensive assessment of 565 nonviolent and violent campaigns between 1900 and 2019 from around the world found that nonviolent campaigns had more than twice the success rate of armed insurrections, even against militarized authoritarian regimes. As noted by Harvard University's Erica Chenoweth:

Contrary to popular belief, it is not the case that nonviolent campaigns emerge or win out mainly when the regimes they confront are politically weak, incompetent, or unwilling to employ mass violence. Once a mass movement arises and unsettles the status quo, most regimes confront unarmed protesters with brute force, only to see even larger numbers of demonstrators turn out to protest the brutality.[3]

As recognition of its potency grows—from Sudan to India and Belarus to Hong Kong—civil resistance has become the strategy of choice for populations who understand that their strongest option is to fight

7

through nonviolent means. Protests in these and many other places are the most visible surface of what is going on, but journalists should also take note of the organizing and coalition building that undergirds these mobilizations, as well as less conspicuous or photogenic acts of omission, which can force concessions by powerholders who are often ill-equipped to handle the collective withdrawal of obedience.

A case in point: In 2019, people in Puerto Rico used widespread, coordinated work stoppages to protest their governor's alleged failures in protecting and assisting the island's many victims of Hurricane Maria. That action, coupled with mass demonstrations, forced Governor Ricardo A. Rosselló to resign in July.

In 2020, protestors in Bolivia added strikes and blockades to their regimen of marches and rallies to pressure their government for the democratic presidential elections they had been promised. After one year of unrelenting protests, the people's "Pitita Revolution" forced an election, resulting in the landslide victory for Luis Arce as the country's new president.

DIVE DEEPER:
WHAT LIES BENEATH

JOURNALISTS USUALLY PROVIDE media coverage when thousands of people publicly protest a powerholder's oppressive policy, practice, or action. The sights and sounds of mass demonstrations hold redoubtable news value.

But rapid, event-driven reporting too often misses information about developments and circumstances that prompted the protests. Additionally, news audiences are not always apprised of other acts of civil resistance that preceded or accompany the visible demonstration — including tactics such as petition drives, work slowdowns, boycotts — as well as the meetings, planning sessions, and coalition-building efforts that are essential to movement success. These nuts and bolts of organizing answer the question of *how* a particular event came to be, and also begin to answer *what a particular event means* for the audience.

Thus, a deeper understanding of the underlying actors, grievances, coalitions, and organizing strategy enables journalists to interpret not just what events are *happening*, but also where events are *going* — to discern whether a big demonstration is merely an attention-grabbing "one-off" event, a spontaneous eruption, or part of a larger and ongoing struggle for rights, freedom, or justice.

Crucially, such context also enables audiences to be less susceptible to the misinformation and agenda-driven framing that fosters misjudgments about the history, motives and actions of the parties involved.

For example, the dramatic nonviolent occupation of Tahrir Square in Cairo, as well as mobilization in other cities across Egypt in early 2011, may have seemed primarily like a spontaneous eruption, as if thousands of long-wronged citizens just snapped. While there was an element of spontaneous participation in those events, other aspects

Few journalists
seemed to know
about the organizers'
commitment to
nonviolent conflict.

of the public mobilization and broader pro-democracy movement were deliberately planned and the outgrowth of years of experience and skill-building among activists. Egyptian activists had staged a litany of civil resistance campaigns long before they took to the streets in such numbers. These earlier organizing efforts included the *Kefaya* ["Enough"] campaign that began in 2003, mobilizing against corruption, and the April 6 movement that began in 2008. Furthermore, activists had prepared for the demonstration against President Hosni Mubarak's government by studying civil resistance literature, sharing knowledge with activists in Tunisia — progenitors of the Arab Spring — and learning from others, such as former members of the Serbian *Otpor* ("Resistance") movement that toppled Serbian President Slobodan Milosevic in 2000. Egyptian activists even developed their own detailed organizing plan to build a mass demonstration in Tahrir Square and overcome the regime's extensive use of riot police.

Many were drawn to the demonstration by social media or word-of-mouth, but it was not mere happenstance, impulse, or raw anger that filled Tahrir Square. Journalists were generally good about reporting the backstory of the long-term abuses, constraints, corruption, and injustices behind the uprising, but few seemed to know about the organizers' commitment to and preparation for nonviolent conflict. As civil resistance expert Hardy Merriman has emphasized, protests and other actions such as we saw in Egypt are not just the work of *activism* but also the work of specific *activists* and *planning*. If such activists can be identified by journalists, assuming they are willing to speak publicly, they can provide deep insight into how the organizing happened and what may come next.[4]

WHEN THINGS GO AWRY

SOMETIMES, A CIVIL RESISTANCE event is marred by violence or significant acts of property destruction. Someone physically harms another, or he or she damages someone else's property. Should the event then be labeled as "violent?"

In the civil resistance lexicon, "nonviolent" means not threatening or inflicting physical harm on another person, and "violent" means the opposite. By that definition, property damage or destruction, looting, flag-burning and the like do not constitute violence, although the fallout from such actions is often similar to that of violence. Therefore, for the sake of accuracy, it's important that journalists distinguish between protesters engaging in property destruction and protesters engaging in violence.

While no one expects media to ignore violence or property destruction, such situations beg context. The proverbial "outside agitator" is a real thing. It may be someone who sympathizes with the activist group but does not share its nonviolent discipline. Or it could be someone who wants to sabotage the action, discredit the host group, and provoke violent reactions from either or both sides. Consider these two examples:

1. August 2007: Canadian Prime Minister Stephen Harper, U.S. President George W. Bush, and Mexican President Felipe Calderon convened a two-day trade summit in Ottawa. More than 1,000 people showed up to peacefully protest the terms of a trilateral pact.

News footage of the crowd shows three men wearing bandanas over their faces pushing toward a line of police in riot gear. Spotting them, protest leaders ask the men to remove their masks and leave the protest. They also order one of the masked men to drop the rock he is carrying. The masked men refuse to comply and press on until they are nabbed by police and handcuffed.

Not only did protest organizers deny knowing the three men, but they also accused the purported strangers of being infiltrators planted by police. Their suspicions were bolstered after a retired Ottawa police officer viewed the video and concluded that "if [the three masked men] weren't police, I think they might well have been working in the best interests of police."

Reviewing the news footage, another activist group noted that the three marauders were wearing the same boots as the riot police — police-issue footwear — lending even more credence to the theory that the men purposefully injected menace and ignominy into an episode of nonviolent civil resistance.[5]

2. May 2020: On the second day of demonstrations in the wake of George Floyd's death at the hands of the Minneapolis police, a masked man with an umbrella was seen smashing storefront windows and spray-painting an invitation to loot the store. The subsequent looting spawned days of rioting. That development dominated coverage, overwhelming the peaceful demonstrations.

Acting on a tip, local police later determined that the mysterious "Umbrella Man" was tied to a white supremacist group seeking to provoke violence and incite interracial conflict.[6]

Both instances required keen- and clear-eyed reporting to prevent a nonviolent campaign from being wrongly blamed for the behavior (and schemes) of either agents provocateurs or rogue activists who abandoned the movement's nonviolent strategy. The coincidence of violent action alongside a campaign that has avowed a nonviolent strategy signals that the journalist has some digging to do.

Getting to the bottom of this can be tricky, requiring the journalist to look beyond the act per se—e.g., "one of the demonstrators struck a police officer with a bottle"—and to re-tell an accurate sequence of events. It also raises the need to discern whether the perpetrator was truly supportive of the protesting group and, if so, whether he or she simply showed up to participate in the action or was part of a more committed planning group that had invested their time and energy in organizing the action. Why is that important? Because it is unfair to report that a group of 200 peaceful marchers "suddenly turned violent" based on the actions of a single violator who "went rogue," a small group of violators, or opportunists with their own agenda whom organizers did not know.

The coincidence of
violent action alongside a
campaign that has avowed
a nonviolent strategy
signals that the journalist
has some digging to do.

A CHECKLIST FOR INCISIVE REPORTING

HERE ARE SOME questions journalists might ask when diving beneath the surface of a civil resistance action and an opponent's reaction:

1. Determining whether it is a movement, a moment or just a mass

Is the mobilized group unified around clearly defined objectives and demands?

What other actions has the group taken?

Is there evidence that different groups are working in coalition?

Are there signs that mobilization and popular participation is growing over time?

Beyond the current action, are other civil resistance actions planned or anticipated?

2. Verifying the movement's commitment to civil resistance

Have the movement's past actions been nonviolent?

Does the movement train its supporters and participants in nonviolent resistance?

Does the movement openly express its commitment to nonviolent resistance? Or is the movement simply choosing nonviolent tactics in a given moment, but leaving open the possibility of adopting a "diversity of tactics," including attacks on persons or property, in the future?

Does the movement have a code of conduct and clear principles of how it functions and that guide its actions?

3. Change in signals

Have the powerholders' efforts to control, rhetorically attack, or repress the movement escalated or diminished? If so, is this happening in size, breadth, or degree? Based on your assessment of other indicators, do these escalatory or de-escalatory actions by powerholders signify weakness and panic or confidence and strength?

Are the powerholders' attempts at repression backfiring by increasing public sympathy for the movement, increasing mobilization in support of the movement, and/or dividing the powerholders' support base?

Do the powerholders' past loyalists and enforcers—e.g., members of the judiciary, state media, strike breakers, trackers, hecklers, police, or military—appear reluctant or enthusiastic in carrying out orders against the movement?

Are there cracks appearing in the powerholders' support base? Have any of the powerholders' pillars of support—e.g., donors, partners, businesses, bureaucrats, members of security forces, or previously allied governments—voiced dissent, become hesitant, or withdrawn their support?

Has either the powerholder or the movement made any concessions to the other?

Dive beneath the surface

CRITIQUE OF SAMPLE
NEWS ARTICLES

EXCELLENT REPORTING ON civil resistance movements defines members of the movement—and not just members of the existing power structure—as primary actors in the story. It allows established organizers and leadership within the movement to articulate the group's goals and motivations and does not rely heavily on bystanders' observations or retaliatory critiques from those within the existing power structure to define the movement. It provides historical context for the movement and situates key events within a timeline. Perhaps most importantly, it does not assume that political power is fixed, based on material and top-down control. Rather, it recognizes that ordinary people have the power to shape events when they unify and engage in civil resistance. Politicians are the ones who ultimately negotiate to pass policy or legislation, but movements change the conditions in ways that make this possible or inevitable.

EXCELLENT coverage also names demonstrations as "peaceful" or "nonviolent" when appropriate and substantiates this by mentioning existing statements, organizations, and/or systems of order that the movement has in place to maintain nonviolent discipline. Such coverage recognizes the impact of such efforts. It does not assume that restraint by the current power structure is responsible for the movement's successes.

If violence occurs, accurate coverage further names the perpetrators. It does not default to describing such events simply as "violent protests," which obscures understanding by leaving readers to guess or project their own biases about who the main perpetrators were and the chain of events. Excellent coverage states clearly if violence is committed against nonviolent resisters, or if a group of unaffiliated people show up to engage in violence alongside protesters. These distinctions are important not only for the sake of accuracy, but they also have significant ramifications for how the story is likely to advance.

AVERAGE coverage discusses actors within the movement but does not recognize them as capable of exercising power. Instead, it assumes that power resides primarily with key powerholders and institutions, and therefore portrays activists as petitioning, pleading, and complaining to try to get attention the attention of powerholders.

The observations of bystanders and/or comments from people who are not fully engaged in the struggle are given outsized weight in defining the movement, and little effort is made to locate and speak with key organizers. The coverage offers some context but also does not fully situate the movement within history or culture. The goals and strategy of the movement are not articulated with clarity and precision.

POOR coverage defines the movement primarily by its acts of disruption and does little to explain the strategy or purpose behind movement demonstrations. It is entirely event driven. Statements from powerholders and outside "experts" are relied on to characterize the movement. Bizarre or unique occurrences are also featured prominently in this type of coverage, and comments from those not fully engaged in the struggle will be used to define it.

Acts of violence by the movement's adversary are not clearly identified as such, and instead lost in vague terminology about "protests turning violent."

Poor movement reporting situates the movement solely against the existing power structure and focuses almost exclusively on points of conflict between the two, ignoring the contextual elements of planning, mobilization, and prior actions.

EXAMPLES OF CIVIL RESISTANCE COVERAGE

Black Lives Matter
2020

Extinction Rebellion
2019

Hirak Movement in Algeria
2019

Armenia's Velvet Revolution
2018

Dakota Access Pipeline
2016

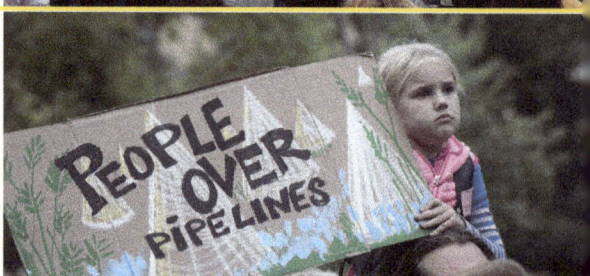

EXCELLENT	AVERAGE	POOR
https://www.nytimes.com/2020/07/19/us/portland-protests.html		https://www.cnn.com/2020/09/27/us/portland-protests-proud-boys-antifa-blm/index.html
https://www.vox.com/energy-and-environment/2019/4/24/18511491/climate-change-protests-london-extinction-rebellion	https://www.theguardian.com/environment/2019/apr/23/labour-extinction-rebellion-climate-change	https://www.reuters.com/article/us-britain-protests-climate-change/climate-change-protesters-target-london-stock-exchange-and-canary-wharf-idUSKCN1S10J5
		https://www.theguardian.com/world/2019/feb/25/algerian-rally-against-president-abdelaziz-bouteflika-plan-seek-fifth-term
https://www.washingtonpost.com/news/monkey-cage/wp/2018/04/30/armenian-protesters-brought-down-a-prime-minister-heres-why-theyre-in-the-streets	https://www.bbc.com/news/world-europe-43948181	https://www.egypttoday.com/Article/1/49160/Protesters-block-roads-across-Armenia-in-stand-off-with-authorities
https://www.nytimes.com/2016/11/29/us/veterans-to-serve-as-human-shields-for-pipeline-protesters.html		

Civil resistance is a technique by which people wage a collective struggle without the use or threat of physical violence.

A GLOSSARY OF CIVIL RESISTANCE TERMS

THE FOLLOWING ARE TERMS commonly used in the field of civil resistance. The definitions in the following three subsections are either directly excerpted from or based upon the *Glossary of Civil Resistance: A Resource for Study and Translation of Key Terms* by Hardy Merriman and Nicola Barrach-Yousefi, which is freely available on the ICNC website as a reference for more than 150 key terms.[7]

Backfire: The concept that a smaller, weaker person can successfully defend against a bigger, stronger assailant by using proper technique and leverage to defeat the opponent (such as using the opponent's weight against him). Although scholar Gene Sharp referred to this phenomenon as "political jiu-jitsu," backfire is the more commonly used term in the field of civil resistance, as popularized by the work of Brian Martin, who developed a five-step process by which movements can cause repression to backfire.

Alternative (or Parallel) Institution: An unofficial institution created by activists to replace or substitute for an existing official institution. It is designed to model or achieve the kind of institution activists have demanded of powerholders. It may also be used to replace a failed or objectionable institution or service, such as in the case of the historic Montgomery Bus Boycott in 1955-56. In that instance, carpools became the alternative to segregated city buses. Such structures are independent of official social, cultural, economic, or government institutions. Alternative or parallel institutions can help a movement function, build and sustain its capacity, support its tactics, increase its self-reliance and legitimacy, and provide for the needs of its supporters.

Constructive Program: The plan for activities and work originated by Mohandas Gandhi for the development of a new social order through voluntary activities and organizations independent of the state and of other established institutions.

Dilemma Action: An act of civil resistance that leaves a powerholder with a Hobson's choice: Either the powerholder capitulates to the resisters' demands or it represses them, which would increase public sympathy for the resisters, and possibly lead to defections among the powerholder's allies and pillars of support.

People Power: The powerful capacity of a mobilized population using nonviolent forms of struggle to make political and social change. The term is sometimes used in civil resistance literature as a synonym for nonviolent struggle and civil resistance. It was first used in 1986 in the Philippines to describe the outpouring of popular opposition and mass demonstrations against the dictator Ferdinand Marcos.

Powerholder: Any entity that decisively affects or controls the liberties, opportunities, policies, and quality and/or conditions of people's lives, whether in a particular circumstance or continually. A powerholder may be public or private, individual or institutional, formal or informal, and a temporary or permanent fixture.

Strategic Nonviolent Struggle: Deliberately planned, disciplined, and targeted waging of conflict by a movement or campaign using strong forms of nonviolent action, especially against powerful and resourceful opponents who may respond with repression.

Tactic of Concentration: A tactic of nonviolent action in which participants or resources are all densely situated in the same place at the same time. Examples of tactics of concentration include mass demonstrations, sit-ins, marches, and rallies. Tactics of concentration tend to be public, exhibit courage, and may be evidence of strong and wide support for a cause. They also tend to be more susceptible to repression than other tactics.

Tactic of Dispersion: A tactic of nonviolent action in which participants or resources are dispersed in many different locations, and/or at many different times. Examples of tactics of dispersion include consumer boycotts and stay-at-home strikes.

Tactical Sequencing: The planned progression of nonviolent tactics, with the aim of achieving a goal, often by escalating pressure on a movement's opponent. Strategic planning in civil resistance often involves the development of sequences of tactics to increase the intensity and range of ways that the movement can pressure its opponent. Because tactics often change as a sequence develops, tactical sequencing and tactical innovation (which refers to the development of new tactics or the modification of existing tactics) are often related.

FAMILIAR TERMS WITH SPECIAL MEANING IN CIVIL RESISTANCE

The following terms have a unique or specialized meaning in civil resistance that may differ from common or intuitive meaning.

Act of Commission: Civil resistance activity in which a person or group does things they usually do not do, are not expected by custom to do, or are forbidden by law or regulation from doing. In the field of civil resistance, an act of commission is always intentional. This makes its meaning narrower than in general English usage, where an act of commission could also be unintentional.

Act of Omission: An act of civil resistance in which a person or group refuses to do things they usually do, are expected by custom to do, or are required by law or policy to do so. Examples of acts of omission include labor strikes, boycotts of all kinds, refusal to pay taxes or utility bills, withdrawal of deposits and investments, and refusal to commemorate or celebrate public or religious holidays. In the field of civil resistance, an act of omission is always intentional. This makes its meaning narrower than in general English usage, where an act of omission could also be unintentional.

Consent: In ordinary usage, the term "consent" in English connotes agreeability—an affirmative statement or action connoting accordance or permission. However, in civil resistance literature the term "consent" is often used in a political context and frequently refers to carrying out orders and the absence of resistance or dissent. In civil resistance literature, the meaning of "consent" is similar to the meaning of "obey" or "acquiesce."

Disruption: A key concept in civil resistance strategy is that nonviolent disruption (i.e., from strikes, boycotts, demonstrations, and many other tactics) imposes costs on oppressive systems. In the face of such actions, it becomes more costly for oppressors to maintain the status quo and continue their oppression. When seen in this regard, disruption can take many forms—it can be chaotic or peaceful, public or invisible, obvious or subtle. For example, a protest or nonviolent occupation of a building are overt and visible forms of disruption, and they may be conducted in a peaceful manner or a loud and aggressive manner. A consumer boycott is a subtle, peaceful, and less visible form of disruption that can nonetheless be immensely powerful.

Failure: In civil resistance literature, the noun "failure" relates to a decisive lack of achievement of a clearly stated goal (or in some cases multiple goals) by a movement. For example, if a movement sets out to change a government policy to achieve a certain outcome, the movement fails or is regarded as a "failure" if it is unable to change that policy in order to achieve its desired outcome. If the movement only partially achieves its goal (or if the movement has multiple goals and achieves only some of them), the movement can be called a "partial success." If the movement achieves its stated goals, it is called a "success."

Force: Conventional usage of this term regarding "use of force" refers to use of violence. However, civil resistance exerts genuine power and force against its adversaries and has been coercive against dictatorships. The way it does this is by eroding the power base of an adversary so that the adversary becomes increasingly isolated and no longer has the capacity to enforce its will.

Success: In civil resistance literature, "success" relates to the achievement of a clearly stated goal (or in some cases multiple goals) by a movement. If the movement only partially achieves its goal (or if the movement has multiple goals and achieves only some of them), the movement can be called a "partial success." If the movement fails to achieve any of its stated goals, it is called a "failure." Some people object to this narrow definition of success, saying that even if a movement fails to achieve its stated objectives, it may succeed at creating other positive effects, and therefore would be deemed a success.

CLARIFYING SOME KEY
CIVIL RESISTANCE TERMS

THE FOLLOWING TERMS are often confused and mistakenly used interchangeably when they actually have different applications:

Activist, Organizer, and Dissident

An **activist** is a person who diligently and repeatedly tries to achieve some social, economic, or political objective, especially by protesting, pressuring, organizing, or resisting. An **organizer** is a person engaged in the planning aspect of participating in a movement, while the term **activist** places the emphasis on the action taken as part of a movement. Most organizers are also activists, but an activist is not necessarily an organizer.

Meanwhile, a **dissident** is a person who has contrary opinions and takes contrary actions to those of the political order and society in which he or she lives. This term was widely used for individuals and groups who opposed Communist Party regimes in the Soviet Union and other Communist strongholds.

Campaign and Movement

A **campaign** has limited objective and duration — i.e., it is a coordinated series of tactics and operations aimed at achieving specific results within a certain timeframe, geography, or political situation. For example, voter registration and lunch counter desegregation were both **campaigns** within the U.S. Civil Rights Movement.

Meanwhile, a **movement** is a large group of people or organizations working together on an ongoing, continual basis, to advance a shared political, economic, and/or social goal. **Movements** are civilian-based, involve widespread popular participation, and alert, educate, serve, and mobilize people to create consequential change. Some key concepts of **movements** are that they:

- Involve popular, voluntary participation of people in a society.
- Involve grassroots participation — they are a bottom-up phenomenon.
- Persist over a period of time.
- Seek to make some form of change (which could be to oppose).

A **movement** may embark on one or more **campaigns** over a period of time.

Civil Resistance and Civil Disobedience

Civil resistance is a technique by which one or more people in a society wage collective nonviolent struggle for political, economic, or social objectives without the use or threat of physical violence.

Civil disobedience defies a particular law or rule and may also represent opposition to wider governmental policies or the government itself. Provided that it is nonviolent, an act of **civil disobedience** can be a method of **civil resistance**.

Tactical Innovation (or Tactical Diversity) and Diversity of Tactics

Tactical innovation refers to a movement adopting new nonviolent tactics over time or performing previously used tactics or methods of civil resistance in new ways. **Tactical innovation** is a key attribute of many successful civil resistance movements. Movements may develop a sequence of tactics that shift over time — for example, a protest, leading to a labor strike, leading to a boycott. Or a movement may perform the same tactics but in a different way—for example, protesting at night, during the day, in different locations, for different durations of time, with large numbers of people, with small numbers of people, etc.

The term **diversity of tactics** may seem to be akin to tactical innovation but surprisingly has a completely different meaning. Diversity of tactics is a term often used by advocates of combining civil resistance, violence, and/or property destruction. It refers to stepping beyond the limits of nonviolent means, but also stopping short of total militarization. Diversity of tactics may promote nonviolent tactics, armed resistance, and/or a range of methods in between, depending on the level of repression the movement is facing.

Loyalty Shift and Defection

These terms are closely related but have notable differences. A **loyalty shift** is the mental or emotional change that happens within an individual or group, which is not always immediately apparent. Civil resistance movements often induce **loyalty shifts** among different individuals and groups in society.

Defection is a conscious decision to withdraw support from a leader or group and/or to take actions to support an opposing leader or group. **Defection** is the consummate indicator of a **loyalty shift**.

Nonviolence and Nonviolent Discipline

Nonviolence is a religious or ethical belief that prohibits violent acts. In some belief systems, only physical violence is disallowed. In other belief systems, hostile thoughts and words may also be forbidden.

Nonviolent discipline is the orderly adherence to the intended course of group activities in a civil resistance campaign, including both compliance with predetermined strategy, tactics, and planned methods of action and maintenance of persistent nonviolent behavior even in the face of repression. A person can practice **nonviolent discipline** without being a disciple of **nonviolence**.

RECOMMENDED READING AND RESOURCES ON CIVIL RESISTANCE

The ICNC Website

A treasury of information about civil resistance including many down-loadable materials: *ICNC Films*; the *"Minds of the Movement"* blog; the *ICNC Interview Series* featuring conversations with some of the world's leading movement organizers, dissidents and researchers; and the *ICNC Resource Library* which contains hundreds of reports, book excepts, articles, research findings, and other materials freely available in over 70 languages and dialects.

How the World is Proving Martin Luther King Right about Nonviolence (newspaper article)

Highlighting findings from their continuing research into civil resistance movements worldwide, researchers Erica Chenoweth and Maria J. Stephan wrote this article for the *Washington Post* in January 2016.

Eight Signs to Identify Nonviolent Conflict (handout)

An ICNC original document, this one-page handout identifies eight signs of emerging strategic nonviolent movements that often occur well before a movement gains widespread media attention.

Correcting Common Misconceptions about Nonviolent Action (book excerpt)

Authored by Gene Sharp, one of the most widely recognized names in the field of civil resistance, this one-page excerpt drawn from *The Politics of Nonviolent Action* provides a succinct definition of nonviolent action and, importantly, clearly establishes what nonviolent action *is not*.

Delivering the Story: Why Movement Reporting Matters (blog post)

Former journalist Deborah Mathis identifies some of the challenges mainstream media face when reporting on nonviolent movements and campaigns and offers a path forward for journalists seeking to go beyond "events" and "effects" to engage the "issues" and "causes."

The Trifecta of Civil Resistance: Unity, Planning, Discipline (online article)

This brief article, originally published on opendemocracy.net in 2010, has been translated into more than 25 languages and widely circulated among seasoned practitioners and newcomers to the field of civil resistance alike. It provides brief summaries of key, historical nonviolent movements, and offers a general framework through which members and supporters of movements, as well as those who report and study them, can quickly assess a movement's state.

198 Methods of Nonviolent Action (webpage)

Adapted from Gene Sharp's 1973 book *The Politics of Nonviolent Action Part II*, this webpage lists 198 of the "nonviolent weapons" that practitioners of nonviolent struggle have at their disposal. These tactics are classified into three broad categories: nonviolent protest and persuasion, noncooperation (social, economic, and political), and nonviolent intervention.

An Outsider's Guide to Supporting Nonviolent Resistance to Dictatorship (full-length report)

In November 2011, a group of experts on nonviolence from around the world gathered in New York to consider how those outside a country subject to dictatorship or repression might help those within it fighting for democracy. The result was this document, a list of nonviolent techniques that can and have been used against repressive dictatorships and autocratic regimes around the world.

WEBINARS AND MULTIMEDIA

Swallowing Camels: How the Media Misinterpret Nonviolent Struggles

This webinar analyzes some of the common ways in which mainstream media coverage of nonviolent struggles and civil resistance tends to reinforce key distortions about these struggles and often unintentionally defaults to the perspective of the oppressor. Suggestions are made for ways in which conscious citizens, activists, and media audiences can help counter these misconceptions.

Conventional Media and Civil Resistance (Fletcher Summer Institute session)

Presented at the Fletcher Summer Institute at Tufts University in 2011, this session provides an in-depth exploration of common media frames and biases that have often led to the distortion of civil resistance movements. It also examines strategies developed by two groups of journalists in different parts of the world struggling to reach their audiences in the face of severe repression.

Global Nonviolent Action Database

This database is a project of Swarthmore College and includes summaries of more than 1,000 nonviolent campaigns worldwide, all of which have reached completion. It is important to note that the case studies included are campaigns and not entire movements. For example, the Civil Rights Movement does not appear, but major episodes of the movement, such as the Montgomery Bus Boycott and the Nashville Sit-ins of 1960, are included.

ENDNOTES

1 Erica Chenoweth and Maria J. Stephan, *"The Future of Nonviolent Resistance," Journal of Democracy* 31, no. 3 (2000).

2 Gene Sharp, *The Politics of Nonviolent Action, Part 2* (Boston: Extending Horizon Books, 1973).

3 Chenoweth and Stephan, *"The Future of Nonviolent Resistance,"* 74.

4 Hardy Merriman, *"Lessons of Uprisings around the World,"* ICNC, Minds of the Movement blog, November 21, 2019.

5 *"Undercover cops tried to incite violence in Montebello: union leader," Canadian Broadcasting Corporation*, CBC.ca, August 22, 2007.

6 Neil MacFarquhar, *"Minneapolis Police Link 'Umbrella Man' To White Supremacy Group," The New York Times*, July 30, 2020.

7 Hardy Merriman and Nicola Barrach-Yousefi, *Glossary of Civil Resistance: A Resource for Study and Translation of Key Terms,* (Washington DC: ICNC Press, 2021).

PHOTO CREDITS

ICNC International Center
on Nonviolent Conflict

CONTACT US

ICNC stands ready to help journalists explain civil resistance so that their readers, viewers, and listeners have a more accurate and clearer understanding of the discipline generally and of developments in the news.

Our staff experts, academic advisors, and colleagues in the field are among the world's leading authorities on civil resistance and its widespread exercise around the world. We look at movements for democratic rights; self-determination; women's and minority rights; transparency (anti-corruption); labor rights; peace and security; economic justice; environmental sustainability and justice; and many other causes. We also look at movements confronting governments, corporations, violent non-state actors, or a combination of such actors.

For information, interviews, and analysis, contact **icnc@nonviolent-conflict.org**.

Glossary of Civil Resistance

A RESOURCE FOR STUDY AND TRANSLATION OF KEY TERMS

Hardy Merriman and
Nicola Barrach-Yousefi

Also Available

Glossary of Civil Resistance

A resource for study and translation of key terms, its primary goal is to help with the translation of information on civil resistance from English into other languages. We also believe that non-translators will find value in it, as a great deal can be learned by reading the definitions and commentary on each term.

www.nonviolent-conflict.org/resource/ glossary-of-civil-resistance/

www.ingramcontent.com/pod-product-compliance
Lightning Source LLC
Chambersburg PA
CBHW052124030426
42335CB00025B/3106